Echoes in the Sky

Echoes in the Sky
An Anthology of Aviation Verse From Two World Wars

Edited and Narrated
by
Ronald Dixon

BLANDFORD PRESS
POOLE DORSET

First published in the U.K. 1982 by Blandford Press, Link House, West Street, Poole, Dorset, BH15 1LL

Distributed in the United States by Sterling Publishing Co., Inc., 2 Park Avenue, New York, N.Y. 10016.

British Library Cataloguing in Publication Data

Echoes in the sky.
1. Aeronautics – Poetry 2. English poetry – 20th century
I. Dixon, Ronald
821'.912'080356 PR1195.A/

ISBN 0 7137 1271 6

Typeset by Memo Typography Limited, Nicosia, Cyprus.
Printed by Biddles Ltd., Guildford

CONTENTS

ACKNOWLEDGEMENTS

The Author would like to thank the following for their kind assistance and the courtesy shown to him in the preparation of this book: Mr C.F.G. Clout, Imperial War Museum; Mr P.G. Dickinson, Fairey Holdings Ltd.; The Librarian and Staff, Adastral Library; Mr A.W.L. Naylor, The Royal Aeronautical Society; Lt. Col. E.M. Solander, U.S.A.F.

★ ★ ★

"The Joy of Flying", by Paul Bewsher, reprinted by permission of Hodder and Stoughton Ltd., from *The Bombing of Bruges* by Paul Bewsher.
"They Called Them R.A.F. 2C's" from *Air Stories*, George Newnes Ltd., London, reprinted by permission of I.P.C.
"The Song of '54' ", from *Air Stories*, George Newnes Ltd., London, reprinted by permission of I.P.C.
"The Nieuport Pilot's Hymn of Hate", from *Air Stories*, George Newnes Ltd., London, reprinted by permission of I.P.C.
"An Irish Airman Foresees His Death", by William Butler Yeats, reprinted by permission of M. B. Yeats, Anne Yeats and Macmillan, London Ltd.
"Every Little While", reprinted by permission of C. H. Ward Jackson, from *Airman's Song Book*, William Blackwood & Sons Ltd., Edinburgh (1967, 2nd edition).
"The Machine Gun", by Goderic Hodges, reprinted by permission of Goderic Hodges and William Kimber & Co. Ltd., from *Memoirs of an Old Balloonatic* by Goderic Hodges.
"A Squadron Song", and "The Low Reconn.", reprinted by permission of Arms ad Armour Press, London, from *Flying Minnows*, by "Roger Vee" (Vivian Voss), (1977).
"A Poor Aviator Lay Dying", from *Air Stories*, George Newness Ltd., London, reprinted by permission of I.P.C.
"All That We Are", reprinted by permission of John Murray (Publishers) Ltd., from *Air Men O'War*, by Boyd Cabee, John Murray, London, 1918.
"R.A.F. - The Ancestors", by C. Day Lewis, reprinted by permission of A. D. Peters & Co., Ltd., from *Per Ardua — The Rise of British Air Power*, by Hilary St. George Saunders, Oxford University Press, 1944.
"The Airman Demobbed", by Cuthbert Hicks, reprinted by permission of Royal Air Force College Cranwell from *Icarus, an Anthology of Flight*, edited by Rupert de la Bere (1938).

"The Desert Mail" by Robert Jope Slade, from *The Aeroplane*, reprinted by permission of I.P.C.
"The 'Peace' of Waziristan", by R. H. Peel, reprinted by permission of C. H. Ward Jackson, from *Airman's Song Book,* William Blackwood & Sons Ltd., Edinburgh (1967, 2nd edition).
"No. 60's D.H.10's", reprinted by permission of Squadron Leader A. J. Young and Flight Lieutenant D. W. Warner, from *Sixty Squadron: 1916 Royal Flying Corps — Royal Air Force 1966: a history of fifty years service,* by A. J. Young and D. W. Warner, published privately in Singapore, 1967; originally from the No. 97 Squadron (re-numbered 60 in 1920) magazine.
"That Old Fashioned Avro of Mine", reprinted by permission of C. H. Ward Jackson, from *Airman's Song Book,* William Blackwood & Sons Ltd., Edinburgh (1967, 2nd edition).
"Sky Fever", by Flight Cadet Percy Robert Hatfield, reprinted by permission of Royal Air Force College Cranwell from *The Journal of the R.A.F. College Cranwell,* Spring 1936.
"We Don't Want To Join The Air Force", reprinted by permission of C. H. Ward Jackson, from *Airman's Song Book,* William Blackwood & Sons, Ltd., Edinburgh (1967, 2nd edition).
"Airmen From Overseas", by Laurence Binyon, reprinted by permission of Mrs. Nicolete Gray and The Society of Authors on behalf of the Lawrence Binyon Estate.
"Passing of a Hurricane", by Pilot Officer O. C. Chave ("Ariel"), reprinted by permission of *Punch*.
"War", by Flying Officer Archibald Nigel Charles Weir, D.F.C., reprinted by permission of Faber and Faber, London, from *Verses of a Fighter Pilot,* by Flying Officer A. N. C. Weir.
"The Flying Instructor's Lament", reprinted by permission of *Punch*.
"If I Only Had Wings", by Sid Collins and Ronnie Aldrich; © Peter Maurice Music Co. Ltd.
"Security", and "For Johnny", by John Pudney, reprinted by permission of The Bodley Head, London, from *Selected Poems,* by John Pudney.
"Operations Calling", by David Bourne, reprinted by permission of The Bodley Head, from *Poems,* by David Bourne.
"Epilogue", by James Gordon, reprinted by permission of Arthur H. Stockwell Ltd., from *Epitaph for a Squadron*.
"When A Beau Goes In", by Gavin Ewart, reprinted by permission of the author.
"The Pilot's Paradise", by Pilot Officer O. C. Chave, (O. C. C.), reprinted by permission of Hutchinson & Co. Ltd., from *Seven Pilots,* by Charles Graves, 1944.
"Swordfish", by R.C. Scriven, reprinted by permission of *Punch*.

"A Young English Airman", by John Masefield, reprinted by permission of The Society of Authors as the literary representative of the Estate of John Masefield.
"Empty Stringbag on the Safi Strip", reprinted by permission of MacDonald and Jane's, London, from *Night Strike From Malta: 830 Squadron, RN, and Rommel's Convoys,* by Kenneth Poolman, 1980.
"The U. S. Air Force", by Robert Crawford, Copyright © 1939, 1942, 1951 by Carl Fisher, Inc., New York. Copyright renewed. Used by permission of Carl Fisher, Inc., New York.
"Epitaph for Flt/Lt Jean 'Peiker' Offenberg, D.F.C.," by Frank H. Zeigler, reprinted by permission of MacDonald and Jane's from *Rendezvous with Fate.*
"Fulmar II", reprinted by permission of Michael Joseph Ltd., from *Tumult in the Clouds,* by John Hoare.
"The Benghazi Mail Run", reprinted by permission of C. H. Ward Jackson from *Airman's Song Book,* William Blackwood & Sons Ltd., Edinburgh (1967, 2nd edition).
"Richard Hillary", by C. A. A., reprinted by permission of Macmillan, London and Basingstoke, from *The Last Enemy,* 1943.
"Sons of the Lords of the Air", by Dick Hurran, © 1943 Peter Maurice Music Co. Ltd.
"That Thing", reprinted by permission of *Aeroplane Monthly,* I.P.C., Sutton, Surrey (June 1979 issue).
"Night Bombers", reprinted by permission of *Punch.*
"The Gallant Sixty-Two", reprinted by permission of C. H. Ward Jackson, from *Airman's Song Book,* William Blackwood & Sons, Ltd., Edinburgh (1967, 2nd edition).
Whilst every effort has been made, the publishers apologise to those whom they have been unable to trace before this book went to press.

* * *

Dedicated to all those
whose words live on as
echoes in the sky

WINGS OF WAR 1914-1918

Little publicity was given to the aviators of the First World War at the time and, with a few exceptions, it was not until some time after the war that the public learned of the exploits of the original 'Hell's Angels' but, once told, their deeds gripped the imagination and have never let go, and there are probably more 'students' of this period now than ever before.

The reason for this interest is easily understood. This war, on the Western Front in particular, was unlike all previous wars in that there had never before been such a hideous slaughter of young men of all armies, under such appalling conditions. It was The Great War to the generation who fought it. In contrast, therefore, the combats, with much smaller casualty lists, that were fought under the blue dome of Heaven were — to those who never fought them — clean, honourable duels which suggested a re-incarnation of the knights of old, complete with their heraldry, who, if they lost their aerial joust, fell to a quick clean death as opposed to the lot of their less fortunate brothers who lay dying and maimed in the blood-soaked mud far below. The truth is, of course, that airmen often suffered equally terrible deaths in blazing aircraft or when structural failure occurred at great heights; for it was deemed — by some who did not fly — that parachutes should not be issued to aircrews for fear that they might be tempted to use them when it was not absolutely necessary! A base slander that was answered not by words, but deeds.

It can be fairly stated, with no disrespect to their German opponents, who fought to the bitter end, that the men of the R.F.C. and R.N.A.S. in particular faced other disadvantages in addition to the accepted hazards of their profession.

First, they flew some types of aircraft, particularly the B.E.2C and R.E.8, which were out-classed by the machines of their opponents and which should have been withdrawn from service long before they were, but remained to increase the casualty lists. Secondly, the official policy which stated that the R.F.C. must always take the fight to the enemy meant that the enemy could, and very often did, choose the 'battlefield', usually well over his side of the lines. The third handicap was the prevailing wind which blew from the Allied lines to the German side and meant that the R.F.C. almost always faced a headwind when returning to their airfields. And so it was that pilots, running low on petrol and ammunition had to fight the wind as well as their opponents, judging when to break off combat and run for home, whereas the enemy could, if he wished, fight until his fuel was nearly exhausted and then make a forced-landing in friendly territory. Because of this there were many more R.F.C. than there were German air services airmen who became prisoners of war.

As a direct result of these disadvantages plus, of course, the fighting abilities of their adversaries, the British losses were at times very high, particularly in that black month which became known as 'Bloody April' (1917). This meant that replacements were rushed to the front with very few hours on the machines that they would fly in combat. It was a particularly vicious circle; the 'new boys' did not last long and were replaced in turn by more new boys. A sad chapter in our air history that was to be repeated twenty-three years later in the Battle of Britain.

History records that, despite their difficulties, the airmen of the British Empire maintained their offensive spirit. These pages record that they also maintained their pride of squadron — and their sense of humour.

The Joy of Flying

One of the original airman/poets, Paul Bewsher's own "Joy of Flying" was marred by the nagging fear that his bombs might kill innocent civilians.

When heavy on my tired mind
  The world, and worldy things, do weigh,
And some sweet solace I would find,
  Into the sky I love to stray,
And, all alone, to wander round
In lone seclusion from the ground.

Ah! Then what solitude is mine —
  From grovelling mankind aloof!
Their road is but a thin-drawn line;
  Their busy house a scarce-seen roof.
That little stain of red and brown
They boast about! — It is their town!

How small their petty quarrels seem!
  Poor, crawling multitudes below;
Which, like the ants, in feverish stream
  From place to place move to and fro!
Like ants they work; like ants they fight,
Assuming blindly they are right.

Soon their existence I forget,
  In joy that on these flashing wings
I cleave the skies — Oh! let them fret —
  Now know I why the skylark sings
Untrammelled in the boundless air —
  For mine it is his bliss to share!

Now do I mount a billowy cloud,
  Now do I sail o'er a hill,
And with a seagull's skill endowed
  Circle, and wheel, and drop at will —
Above the villages asleep,
Above the valleys, shadowed deep,

Above the water-meadows green
  Whose streams, which intermingled flow,
Like silver lattice-work are seen
  Agleam upon the plain below —
Above the woods, whose naked trees
Move new-born buds upon the breeze.

And far away above the haze
  I see white mountain-summits rise
Whose snow with sunlight is ablaze
  And shines against the distant skies.
Such thoughts these towering ranges bring
That I float on a-wondering!

So do I love to travel on
  Through lonely skies, myself alone;
For then the feverish threat is gone
  Which on this earth I oft have known.
Kind is the God who lets me fly
  In sweet seclusion through the sky!

Paul Bewsher,
D.S.C., R.N.A.S.

They Called Them R.A.F. 2C'S

The Royal Aircraft Factory's (R.A.F) B.E.2C was a very stable aeroplane, which made it useless for air combat. Despite this they were still built and used — at a very high cost in life.

Oh! they found a bit of iron what
Some bloke had thrown away,
And the R.A.F. said, "This is just the thing
We've sought for many a day."

They built a weird machine,
The strangest engine ever seen,
And they'd quite forgotten that the thing was rotten,
And they shoved it in a flying machine.

Then they ordered simply thousands more,
And sent them out to fight.
When the blokes who had to fly them swore,
The R.A.F. said, "They're all right
The 'bus is stable as can be;
We invented every bit ourselves, you see!"

They were so darn' slow, they wouldn't go,
And they called them R.A.F. 2C's!

The Pilot's Psalm

Yet another criticism of the R.A.F. B.E.2C and its engine. No irreverence was intended; in fact, the pilot is praying for deliverance from this aircraft!

The B.E.2C is my 'bus; therefore I shall want.
He maketh me to come down in green pastures.
He leadeth me where I will not go.
He maketh me to be sick; he leadeth me astray
  on all cross-country flights.
Yea, though I fly over No-man's land where mine
enemies would compass me about, I fear much evil
for thou art with me; thy joystick and thy prop
  discomfort me.
Thou preparest a crash before me in the presence
of thy enemies; thy R.A.F. anointeth my hair with
  oil, thy tank leaketh badly.
Surely to goodness thou shalt not follow me all
the days of my life; else I shall dwell in the
  House of Colney Hatch forever.

The Song of "54"

This song was sung by the members of No. 54 Squadron, R.F.C., to the well-known tune of "Oh! We've come up from Somerset"

Oh! We came up from Birmingham
To see the great big war,
There was Oxo right chock full of fight,
And Nobby out for gore.
Archie shot at us "gr-r-umph! umph!"
And blacked the sky so blue,
When right up flew a Halberstadt
And said, "And vitch vos you?"

Chorus
Oh, we've come up from Fifty-Four;
We're the Sopwith Pups, you know,
And wherever you crafty Fokkers may be
The Sopwith Pups will go.
And if you want a proper scrap,
Don't chase 2C's any more;
For we'll come up and do the job,
Because we're Fifty-Four!

A two-seater looked at Oxo,
And "Vat vos you?" he said;
And Oxo blushed quite red with rage,
And shot the blighters dead.
Then we found some Hun balloonists
Behind old Vendhuille town;
The huns seemed keen to pull it in,
And so we helped it down.

Chorus
Oh, we've come up from Fifty-Four, etc.

Then the Hun he looked down on to Peronne,
From which he'd run away,
And Struggy, seeing seven there,
Cried, "Splendid! Chaps! Hooray!
Although there's only four of us,
You've got to fight, you see."
And so they went right into them!
By gad! they brought down three!

Chorus
Oh, we've come up from Fifty-Four, etc.

Captain Albert Ball V.C.

Dashing and fearless, Albert Ball, V.C., was one of the few airmen who, deservedly, received publicity. At the time of his death, aged twenty, he was officially credited with forty-four victories.

You may prate of dashing Majors, or of gallant grim old
  stagers
 When you're sitting in the smoke-room of the club;
You may laud the high endeavour of the warriors swift and
  clever,
 From the Colonel to the smallest junior sub.
They are Britain's vowed defenders, they have added to her
  splendours,
 They are heroes in excelsis, one and all;
But the Trojan of our nation, who has soared to fame's high
  station,
 Is the Nottinghamshire nugget — Albert Ball!

He has hewn a path to Glory; he shall live in endless story;
 He has triumphed in the conquest of the air.
He has wrought a thousand wonders 'mid the tumult and
  the thunders
 Of a war with which no other can compare.
He was true to our traditions; he fulfilled the fiercest mis-
  sions
 With a bravery that nothing shall efface;
Bringing Bosches down in plenty, he, a youth of only
  twenty,
 Must be reckoned with the giants of the race!

He is gone from us for ever; yet his fame shall falter never,
And his deeds of dazzling daring shall endure,
To inspire each generation with a glowing admiration
Of the ways of peerless pilots, swift and sure.
Though his innings here is finished, still with fervour undiminished
We will praise him first and foremost in the van;
And wherever men may muster, they shall magnify his lustre,
For he proved himself a pilot and — a Man!

G. R. Samways, R.F.C.

"We Haven't Got a Hope in the Morning"

Another of No. 54 Squadron's songs makes light of their daily problems. Although their Scouts ("Pups") had only one gun and an 80 h.p. engine, their outstanding manoeuvrability made them a first class fighter.

When you soar into the air on a Sopwith Scout,
And you're scrapping with a Hun and your gun cuts out,
Well, you stuff down your nose till your plugs fall out,
'Cos you haven't got a hope in the morning.

Chorus: For a batman woke me from my bed;
I'd had a thick night and a very sore head,
And I said to myself, to myself I said,
"Oh, we haven't got a hope in the morning!"

So I went to the sheds and examined my gun,
Then my engine I tried to run,
And the revs. that it gave were a thousand to one,
'Cos it hadn't got a hope in the morning.

Chorus: For a batman, etc.

We were escorting Twenty-Two,
Hadn't a notion what to do,
So we shot down a Hun and an F.E. too,
'Cos they hadn't got a hope in the morning.

Chorus: For a batman, etc.

We went to Cambrai, all in vain;
The F.E.'s said "We must explain;
Our cameras broke — we must do it again"
"Oh, we haven't got a hope in the morning!"

Chorus: For a batman, etc.

Missing

This poem is dedicated to those unsung heroes of the air, the seaplane crews of the R.N.A.S.

He has gone hence: now therefore he is free
By grace of an invisible city,
Inheritor of a serene air,
Untouched by change of time, uncrazed by care.
He will not now return to those he knew,
He will not fly with those who gaily flew
Into the storm, into the cloud, into the night
He has passed out upon the farthest flight
That ever airman ventures: on and on,
Beyond earthmark or airmark he has gone.
His seaplane, like a swimmer, clave the sea,
And, as she rose, shook off mortality;
Drawn into deeps of being, boundless tides
Of beauty, where no veil or bar divides
Body and spirit, shadow and the light,
Things that are seen and unseen, faith and sight.

E. Vine Hall

The Nieuport Pilot's Hymn of Hate

This was the song of No. 60 Squadron R.F.C., who were equipped with the French "Baby" Nieuport Scouts. It is sung to the tune of "Onward Christian Soldiers"

Onward, Baby Nieuports,
Flying out to war,
Lewis guns all loaded,
Engines all a-roar.
See the Flight Commander
Leads against the foe,
Five machines with engines revving,
Cylinders a-glow.
Onward, Baby Nieuports,
Flying out to war,
Lewis guns all loaded,
Engines all a-roar.

At the sign of triumph
The Wily Hun doth flee,
"Dive then, Baby Nieuports
Dive to victory"
Albatrosses quiver,
Engines glowing red.
Crack ! Crack ! Crack ! behind them,
(Onward, etc.)

See the Albatros's
Tanks begin to leak,
As the guns of Nieuports,
One and all do speak.
Diving ever downwards,
Every Wily Hun,
Into flames they're bursting,
"Nieuports — you have won!"
(Onward, etc.)

Pull your joysticks backwards,
Zoom towards the skies,
Up to fifteen thousand
Fast the Nieuports rise.
Guns once more are silent,
All their rounds are loosed,
Now they're flying westwards —
Flying home to roost.
(Onward, etc.)

Welcome, Bristol Fighters,
Who towards us soar,
Blend with ours your engines,
As we homeward roar.
"We have done much battle
With the Albatross,
Never will they fly again
Now they bite the moss"
Onward, Nieuports, Bristols,
Flying home from war,
With your Flight Commanders
Going on before.

The Call of the Air

This poem did more than tell young men of the thrill of flying; it challenged them to find out for themselves. The poet actually wrote poems whilst flying — probably this one!

Have you ever sat in crystal space, enjoying the sensations
  of an eagle hovered high above the earth,
gazing down on man's ridiculous and infantile creations
  and judging them according to their worth?
Have you looked upon a basin small enough to wash your face in,
  with a few toy ships collected by the shore,
and then realised with wonder that if those toys go under
  nine-tenths of Britain's Navy is no more?

Have you seen a khaki maggot crawling down a thread of cotton —
  the route march of a regiment or so?
Have you seen that narrow riband, unimportant, half-forgotten,
  that tells you that the Thames is far below?
Have you glanced with smiling pity at the world's most famous city,
  a dirty smudge that barely strikes the eye?
Would you like to see things truly and appreciate them duly?
  Well then do it, damn you, do it: learn to fly!

Have you left the ground in murkiness all clammy, grey and
soaking.
and struggled through the dripping, dirty white?
Have you seen the blank sides closing in and felt that you
were choking,
and then leapt into a land of blazing light,
where the burnished sun is shining on the cloud's bright
silver lining,
a land where none but fairy feet have trod,
where the splendour nearly blinds you and the wonder of it
binds you.
and you know you are in heaven, close to God?

Have you tumbled from the sky until your cries were shrilly
screaming,
and watched the earth go spinning round about?
Have you felt the hard air beat your face until your eyes were
streaming?
Have you turned the solar system inside out?
Have you seen earth rush to meet you and the fields spread
out to greet you,
and flung them back to have another try?
Would it fill you with elation to be boss of all creation?
Well then do it, damn you, do it; learn to fly!

Have you fought a dummy battle, diving, twisting, pirouetting,
at a lightning speed that takes away your breath?
Have you been so wildly thrilled that you have found yourself forgetting
that it's practice, not a battle to the death?
Have you hurtled low through narrow, tree-girt spaces like an arrow —
seen things grow and disappear like pricked balloons?
Would you feel the breathless joys of it and hear the thrilling noise of it,
the swish, the roar, the ever-changing tunes?

Have you chased a golden sunbeam down a gold and silver alley,
with pink and orange jewels on the floor?
Have you raced a baby rainbow round a blue and silver valley,
where purple caves throw back the engines roar?
Have you seen the lights that smoulder on a cloud's resplendent shoulder
standing out before a saffron-coloured sky?
Would you be in splendid places and illimitable spaces?
Well then do it, damn you, do it; learn to fly!

Jeffery Day,
D.S.C., R.N.A.S.

The Early Show

The crews of No. 22 Squadron sang their song to the tune of "The Alabama Choo-Choo". However, their record shows that the combats were not as one-sided as the song may suggest!

When the early show sets out to cross the lines,
I'll be right there, I'll do my share.
When we see suspicious 'buses revving east;
We're far too low, that's Von Bulow,
Albatri ! Albatri !
The beggar's on my tail
I'm turning rather pale
My 'bus seems like a snail;
As down I go! Oh!
Why can't that damned Archie stop!
Gee I've been and shot my prop.!
Have a heart — have a heart.
For I'm on the early show.

When that early show gets over to Gontrode,
I'm with them still...(against my will!)
When we see some Black and White ones underneath
We've done it once too often
That's Richtofen
Albatri! Albatri!
He's stalling up at me
And shooting up at me
Why can't the leader see those Huns below? Oh!
Only last one thing I ask,
Where's that wretched brandy flask?
Have a heart — have a heart!
For we're on the early show.

An Irish Airman Forsees His Death

W. B. Yeats wrote this poem in memory of his close friend, Major Robert Gregory, R.F.C. It is also an epitaph for all those Irish airmen killed whilst serving with the British air services.

I know that I shall meet my fate
Somewhere among the clouds above;
Those that I fight I do not hate,
Those that I guard I do not love;
My country is Kiltartan Cross,
My countrymen Kiltartan's poor;
No likely end could bring them loss
Or leave them happier than before.
Nor law, nor duty bade me fight,
Nor public men, nor cheering crowds,
A lonely impulse of delight
Drove to this tumult in the clouds;
I balanced all, brought all to mind,
The years to come seemed waste of breath,
A waste of breath the years behind,
In balance with this life, this death.

William Butler Yeats

The Ballad of the Bristol Fighter

Despite a tragic debut the "Brisfit" soon proved herself to be a magnificent aircraft, feared by the enemy and loved by all who flew and fought in her.

There's a good half-dozen 'buses
On which I've done a whack,
From the R.E.8 to the three-ton weight
Of the lumbering old Big Ack.
On a rotary-engined Avro,
I've attempted several tricks
And I'm quite a dab at steering a Crab
(Better known as a D.H.6.).

And many a first-rate joy-ride
Have I had on 'em last and first,
And many a strut have I had go phut,
And many a wheel tyre burst.
But none of them know the secret
Of making my heart rejoice
Like a well-rigged Bristol Fighter
With a two-six-four Rolls Royce.

She leans at her place on the tarmac
Like a Tiger crouched for a spring,
From the arching spine of her fuselage line
To the ample spread of her wing.
With her tyres like sinews tautened
And her tail-skid's jaunty twist,
Her grey-cowled snout juts grimly out
Like a tight-clenched boxer's fist.

Is there a sweeter music,
A more contenting sound,
Than the purring clop of her broad-curved prop
As it gently ticks around?
Open her out crescendo
To a deep-toned swelling roar,
Till she quivers and rocks as she strains at the chocks
And clamours amain to soar.

Whisk 'em away, my hearties,
Taxi her into the wind,
Then away we skim on a spinning rim
With the tail well up behind;
Hold her down to a hundred,
Then up in a climbing turn
And off we sweep in a speckless sky
Till we catch our breath in the air Alp-high.
I wouldn't exchange my seat, not I,
For a thousand pounds to burn.

H. T. Burt

Every Little While

Retaining the title of a popular song from one of the musical comedies 1917-1918, this light-hearted ditty was a favourite in the Mess.

Every little while I crash a Camel,
Every little while I hit a tree,
I'm always stalling — I'm always falling,
Because I want to fly a posh S.E.
Every little while my engine's conking,
Every little while I catch on fire.
All the time I've got my switch up
I've always got the wind up,
Every, every, little while.

The Machine Gun

The balloon observers were equipped with parachutes, which was a good thing for when enemy fighters attacked them a very quick jump was their only means of survival.

Balloonatics all hate one sound, which is to them
detestable.
It mars for them the pleasures of an afternoon
delectable,
And brings them moments of regret entirely
unforgettable.
It is a brute.

When this is heard, their curses loud proclaim they
are distinctly bored.
They seize their maps, then hastily on either side
leap overboard.
They hurtle earthward, praying hard, suspended
from a hateful cord.
They parachute.

On cloudy days most frequently observers' mind
it agitates.
Then safe approach and sudden dive the crafty Hun
anticipates,
As, flying westward all unseen, his foul designs
he meditates.
Balloons to shoot.

Goderic Hodges

You're Only a P.B.O.

The Poor Bloody Observer rarely received just recognition for his sterling work. In this song, to the tune of "A Bachelor Gay", he tells his sad story.

When you climb in the old machine to start on a damned
O.P.
You cover yourself with tons of clothes and they're all of
them N.B.G.,
The pilot sits near the engine's warmth, his body with heat
aglow,
Whilst you must stand in the back and cuss
Till the ice on your whiskers stalls the bus,
You're only a P.B.O., yes, only a P.B.O.

Chorus

At seventeen thou. he's shooting rather badly at a Pfalz of
tender blue,
At fifteen thou. you see him point out sadly some Huns of a
different hue,
At ten or twelve he's shooting rather madly at six or eight or
more.
When he fancies he is past hope
Fires a long burst as a last hope
And a Hun spins down on fire to the floor!

When you're doing an escort stunt and the Huns get on your tail
You fire and aim till you see 'em flame and down they go like hail.
Alas, the pilot's jealous scorn is a thing we learn to know,
You may get twenty Huns in flames
Don't think that they'll believe your claims,
For you're only a P.B.O., yes, only a P.B.O.

Chorus: At seventeen, etc.,

We all of us know the case when the pilot came home alone,
No doubt it was only a slight mistake, but his attitude's clearly shown.
He suddenly shoved his joystick down as far as it would go.
"Hello, you seem to have gone," he said.
"I fear you must be somewhat dead,
But you're only a P.B.O., yes, only a P.B.O."

Chorus: At seventeen, etc.,

I managed to get my leave, and was trying to drown the past,
When I chanced on a maiden passing fair, and thought I had clicked at last.
To my joy she said "The R.F.C. are the nicest boys I know"
When I said "Well, I'm an Observer, dear,"
She said "There's nothing doing here,
You're merely a P.B.O., a miserable P.B.O."

Chorus: At seventeen, etc.,

Over the Lines

This is a very visual poem: one can almost feel the bumps...see the rest of the Flight rising and falling in the turbulent air...!

We were flying in formation and continued to keep our station,
Though the wind was trying hard to sweep the sky,
And we watched the puffs of powder, heard the Archies booming louder
And we didn't need to stop to reason why.
With the German lines below us, and a gale that seemed to throw us
Into nowhere as it would a schoolboy's kite,
We went skimming through the ether always keeping close together
And we felt the joy of battle grip us tight.

Then from out of the horizon which we kept our eager eyes on
Swept the Fokkers in their deadly fan-wise dash.
Soon the Vickers guns were cracking and a couple started backing,
Whilst a third was sent down flaming in a flash.
How we blessed our Bristol Fighters as we closed in with the blighters,
And we zoomed and banked and raced them through the air.

We abandoned our formation, but we won the situation,
  Won it easily, with four machines to spare.
Then Archie burst around us, and the beggar nearly found us,
  But we dived towards our lines without delay,
And we finished gay and merry from a binge of gin and sherry,
  For we knew we lived to see another day.

A Squadron Song

At a party, after a tremendous dogfight in which ten "Brisfits" claimed eleven plus victories, the aircrews composed this ditty. Squadron M was, in fact, No. 88 Squadron.

Twelve young pilots from (Squadron M),
Took the air one morn at eight,
They met fifty Huns, they say,
Over the middle of Tournai.

Chorus: So early in the morning,
So early in the morning,
So early in the mor-r-r-r-ning,
Before the break of day.

Hep was leading A Flight then,
(Murray) followed with B Flight men,
There were eight old Fokkers in the sun,
That is the way of the wily Hun.

Chorus: So early in the morning, etc.

Hep got a Hun right on his tail,
He did a half-roll without fail,
Then his gun went dud they say,
So he came home and left the fray.

Chorus: So early in the morning, etc.

A Flight followed back to the lines,
And there we met some D.H.9's,
They didn't see any Huns about,
Soon they went like a bloody scout.

Chorus: So early in the morning, etc.

The wily Fokkers climbed aloft,
And thought ha! ha! here's something soft,
But we four Bristols came out of the sun,
And that soon stopped the beggars' fun.

Chorus: So early in the morning, etc.

The P.B.O.s shot well that day,
And every gun got its Hun, they say,
(Trent) fired and kept them away,
While (Grant's) Very lights frightened them away.

Chorus: So early in the morning, etc.

The Low Reconn.

Another song sung in No. 88 Squadron's Mess, to the tune of "What do you want to make those eyes at me for", makes light of their feelings towards the dangers of the low reconnaissance flights they often made.

What do I have to do a low reconn. for,
It's the second time to-day,
It makes me sad,
It makes me mad
To think of all the bolo jobs I might have had!
What do I have to fly below the clouds for,
A thousand feet is quite too bally low!
But never mind, we'll go up again some day,
At eighteen thou' we'll gambol and play.
If I do another show like the last one,
Why, I won't need next month's pay!

A Poor Aviator Lay Dying

This horribly mournful ditty has been sung with gusto by aviators since the earliest days of the R.F.C., to the tune of "My Old Tarpaulin Jacket"

Oh, a poor aviator lay dying
At the end of a bright summer's day,
His comrades were gathered around him
To carry the fragments away.

The engine was piled on his wishbone,
The Hotchkiss was wrapped round his head,
A spark-plug stuck out of each elbow
It was plain that he'd shortly be dead.

He spat out a valve and a gasket
And stirred in the sump where he lay,
And then to his wond'ring comrades,
These brave parting words he did say;

"Take the manifold out of my larynx
And the butterfly valve off my neck,
Remove from my kidneys the camrods,
There's a lot of good parts in this wreck.

"Take the piston rings out of my stomach,
And the cylinders out of my brain,
Extract from my liver the crankshaft,
And assemble the engine again.

"I'll be riding a cloud in the morning
With no rotary before me to cuss,
So shake the lead from your feet and get busy,
There's another lad wanting this 'bus"

Who minds to the dust returning?
Who shrinks from the sable shore?
Where the high and the lofty yearning
Of the soul shall be no more?

So stand to your glasses steady,
This world is a world full of lies,
Here's a health to the dead already,
And hurrah for the next man who dies!

The Ghosts of the Eighth Attack

Sadly, but with obvious pride, this American airman recalls the hectic days and the gallant members of his old squadron.

When first the roar of a D.H.4
  Came sounding over the plain,
The clan who flew were tried and true,
  And sound of heart and brain,
Our Squadron then lost gallant men,
  And well we have learned their lack;
And we'll drink a toast to each brave ghost, —
  The Ghosts of the Eighth Attack.

Kingsland turned to a spin and burned,
  Rex and Gallagher died
In battle flame on the field of fame,
  With Mitchell by their side,
From death unveiled they never quailed,
  Or broke upon the rack,
But well we ken they fought like men,
  The Ghosts of the Eighth Attack!

Dean and Bateman and Hollingsworth —
  Death garnered, thigh and thew,
And Captain Shea, with his Irish way, —
  Virgin and Hartmann too.
Robinson, Martin, Grodecki,
  And Mackey, and Womack;
Brave hearts of gold that now lie cold, —
  The Ghosts of the Eighth Attack

And I sometimes think, when the night winds howl,
  And never a ship is out,
That I hear the roar of a D.H.4,
  And the wail of wires in doubt;
And I think I see in a spectre ship
  Spirits that must come back;
And I hail them then, who have died like men, —
  The Ghosts of the Eighth Attack!

J. L. Hitchings

If You Want to Remain Inside

Again sung to the tune of "A Bachelor Gay" this song humourously gives advice on forced-landings. You vary the speeds according to the type you fly.

When you're flying the old Nine "A" on a bumpy,
windy day,
And your engine begins to splutter out and you
think you have lost your way,
Be careful to keep your head to wind if you want
to reduce your glide,
And sideslip over a downwind fence,
If you want to remain inside your field,
If you want to remain inside, you want to remain inside.

Chorus

At eighty-five you head her in so nicely, a glide
you should not exceed;
At seventy-five you flatten out precisely, and still,
you've got lots of speed;
At sixty-five you pull the stick back gently to put
her on the floor.
But at fifty you'll be stalling,
And you'll realise you're falling,
And you'll crash her as she's never crashed before!

"Seventy Four"

No. 74 (Tiger) Squadron had a star-studded "cast", but the man whom they respected above all others was their C.O., the New Zealand "ace", Major Keith ("Grid") Caldwell, M.C., D.F.C.

In France there's a damn good old Squadron
Though the drome's on the side of a hill,
It's a Squadron of great reputation,
It is Seventy Four escadrille.

There was Mannock of fame in the Air Force,
Hunarinos he shot down with ease,
As happy as hell round the aerodrome,
As he shouted for, "All tickets please".

And Roxburgh, and Taffy and Youngski,
Men who are all in the air,
And all the rest in the Squadron,
The best you could find anywhere.

Now one toast will I offer in closing,
Just one it could easily be more,
A toast to the C.O. who led us,
To Caldwell of Seventy Four.

"All That We Are"

Aircraft of the Corps Wings (Army Co-operation) had the less glamourous tasks of photography, artillery spotting and reconnaissance. It is impossible to estimate the value of their contribution to the final victory.

All that we are and all we own,
All that we have and hold or take,
All that we tackle or do or try
Is not for our, or the Corps' own sake.

Through our open eyes the Armies see,
We look and we learn that they may know.
Collect from the clouds the news they need,
And carry it back to them below.
We harry the guns that do us no harm,
We picture the paths we shall never take;
There's naught to help or to hinder us
On the road we bomb or the bridge we break.
Only to work where our footmen wish,
Only to guard them from prying eyes,
To find and to fetch the word they want,
We war unceasing and hold the skies.

All that we are and all we own,
All that we have or hope or know,
Our work and our wits, our deaths, our lives,
We stake above, that they win below.

Omer Drome

Sung to the tune of "My Old Kentucky Home", this parody makes reference to the much used tightest of turns, a term that many airmen still think of as originating in World War Two!

I've got a windy feeling round my heart
  And it's time that we went home,
I've got a great big longing to depart
  Somewhere back to Omer Drome.
Huns are diving at my tail,
Wind up — Gee! — I've got a gale.
  Guns are jamming,
  Pilots damning,
Archies bursting all around us.
  And observers say,
"Ain't it time that we came down".
So won't you splitass back
Along the track
To my dear old Omer Town.

R.A.F. — The Ancestors

They were the men who dreamed of wings and made that dream reality. They were the men who used those wings in war, and laid the foundations of a great tradition.

Inventive men, haunted by images
Of flight, they worked in power and stress to learn
The swallow's long endurance, the pacific
Gliding of gulls, the plover's looping turn.

Audacious men, they clothed their vibrant vision
With wood and linen, flew it in the teeth
Of gravity, and like enchanters held
A fragile art between themselves and Death.

Air-worthy men, sons of an element
That speaks in light and lifts the venturer high,
They traced a buoyant span from shore to shore
Or fell like sunbursts from the embattled sky.

Their spirit rose in fine pitch off the field
Of earth, taking a steep way to the stars:
History flew beside them, and bright fame
Arches her wings above their cloudy wars.

C. Day Lewis

WINGS OF PEACE, 1919 - 1939

The war to end all wars was over and the Royal Air Force, formed by an amalgamation of the R.F.C. and the R.N.A.S. on 1st April 1918, was, temporarily, unemployed. By the end of the War it had become the world's greatest air force, numbering over 291,000 men of all ranks and some 200 operational squadrons but, with the country's economy in chaos and there being no major enemy (there were some squadrons operating against the Reds in Russia) to justify such a force, the axe had to fall and it did so with such severity that by December 1919 (just over one year since the last Dawn Patrol had been flown) the Service could only muster a mere 36,000 men and less than a score of squadrons!

Although 1919 saw the R.A.F. at its lowest ebb the year was not without its events, for men who had no trade other than aviation were seeking fresh employment for their talents. June witnessed the first trans-atlantic flight by Captain John Alcock and Lieutenant Whitten Brown. In July the airship *R. 34* (Major Scott i/c) flew the Atlantic and back again, and in November the Australian brothers Captain Ross Smith and Lieutenant Keith Smith made the first ever flight to Australia. All were truly epic flights of outstanding navigation and airmanship that set the scene for the many long distance and record breaking flights that followed. The year ended on a brighter note for the R.A.F., however, for in December the then Secretary of State for Air, Mr Winston Churchill, laid before parliament a scheme for the permanent organisation of the R.A.F., a new start for the service.

In February 1920 the R.A.F. College at Cranwell was

opened and by March the number of squadrons had risen to twenty-five with eight more in the process of formation. Slowly the service was beginning to re-build and a very big step forward came in 1922 when the R.A.F. assumed Air Control of Iraq. This policing by air meant that a few squadrons would do the work of thousands of soldiers in a much quicker time. The practice was that rebel tribesmen would first be warned and then bombed, and it worked very well, the casualties on both sides being minimal. Air Control was later operated successfully in Aden, India and the Sudan, and many a large scale uprising was nipped in the bud, with the possible overall saving of thousands of lives.

It was in 1925 that the powers-that-be finally decided that aircrews would wear parachutes! Also in that year the Auxiliary Air Force was formed, various counties each having a squadron. This was a sound investment that paid invaluable dividends in 1940.

Another milestone in the R.A.F's history was reached when they successfully evacuated 586 British persons from the besieged city of Kabul, Afghanistan, between 23rd December 1928 and 25th February 1929, there being a very real danger of them being massacred by rebels.

During all these years aircrews had been making many long-distance flights and continuing the pioneering of air mail/passenger routes, but as far as the public were concerned the next big event was the outright winning of the Schneider Trophy by the Supermarine S 6B in September 1931, having won in 1927 and 1929; three consecutive wins (1928 and 1930 were not run) entitled the winner to the Trophy. That same month saw an S 6B capture the World Speed Record at a fantastic 407.5mph. This was the aircraft that sired the Spitfire.

By 1934 the number of squadrons had risen to forty-two

but the majority of these were equipped with bombers, for the high command believed the bomber to be the ultimate deterrent; they seemed to have overlooked the very real possibility that others may have more bombers — and how were they to be deterred?

Because the Service was small in numbers most of the pilots (at least) knew each other and this resulted in the R.A.F. gaining the unofficial title of "the most exclusive flying club in the world"— which was not far from the truth!

The Service was re-organised into Commands in July 1936 which was a step in the right direction. An even bigger step also taken that month was the formation of the Royal Air Force Volunteer Reserve which, like the Aux. A.F., was to be of incalculable value in just a few years. These moves were not before time, however, for in that year the *Luftwaffe* sent its Condor Legion to fight in the Spanish Civil War which, with typical German thoroughness, they used as an operational training school — and their airmen learned their lessons well!

The sands of peace-time were running out fast but in 1937 Britain's fighter defence still consisted of biplane fighters. Even at the time of the Munich crisis in 1938 only a few units had Hurricanes or Spitfires and the only really efficient bomber was the Wellington. However, the mounting international tension had forced the "ostriches" to withdraw their heads from the sand and Britain joined in the race for aircraft production — albeit several laps behind the rest of the field — and immediately prior to the outbreak of hostilities there were some 500 plus Hurricanes and Spitfires: the race had not been won, but a lot of lost ground had been made up.

1st September 1939, saw the birth of the Air Transport

Auxiliary which took from the Service pilots the additional burden of aircraft ferrying.

On 2nd September a few members of the public on the Sussex coast were treated to an aerial spectacle as ten squadrons of Battle bombers — 160 aircraft — winged their way to France. The proud watchers could not know that these aircraft were under-powered, under-armed and no match for the enemy who they were to face so courageously.... they were a doomed armada.

Initiation

This most profound poem is dedicated to the international brotherhood of airmen who share the freedom of the sky.

That I have lived to see men fly
In remote reaches of the sky,
Ready the darkest hour to dare
In the deep spaces of the air,
To take their station by the stars,
And to stand sentry at the bars
Of sunset; to excel in speed
The very vulture, to exceed
For height the hawk, for grace the gull,
Man's marks and limits to annul,
Till earth shrink to an island, hung
The heaven's other orbs among,
And the world but a shadow seems
Of unintelligible dreams,
Staggers my soul. Therefore I see,
As knit in one society,
Seers, saints and airmen; all who rise
To the pure place of the clear skies
And read, as in a mirror's face,
The hidden things of time and space.

E. Vine Hall

The Airman Demobbed

For the ex-airman the threat of sudden death has gone — but so too has the freedom of flight.

I rode the storm and the lightning
And raced the gay clouds as I flew,
Dipped under the arch of the rainbow,
And swung like a star in the blue.

I slid down the path of the sunbeams,
And swooped like a gull to the wave,
I dropped o'er the crest of the mountains,
Down the streams that the valleys gave.

Now my feet are leaden and earthbound
And I know why the caged bird dies,
For my soul looks out to the blue ways,
When I dare look up at the skies.

Cuthbert Hicks

Laus Deo In Excelsis

When flying under Heaven's blue dome and above an unbroken carpet of purest white one is indeed inclined to "Praise God in the Highest"

The sullen cloud that screens the world below
Changes before my eyes to purest snow,
And peerless napery for mile on mile
Lies laden in the joy of Heaven's smile.
And all the time the little aeroplane
Plays with its shadow on that wondrous plain.
        And as for me, I nod
To mine own image bidden to the feast,
And for that moment, I am not the least
        Of all the Sons of God.

F. MacNeece Foster

The "Peace" of Waziristan

From 1920 onwards a few Squadrons of the R.A.F. policed vast areas of the Middle East and India. It was, militarily, a very economical and effective means of controlling the tribes. It was also dangerous!

"Oh big 9A! Oh big 9A!
What are you doing Razmak way?
Why these bombs, this pomp of war?
Surely your home's in Risalpur?"

"Pomp be damned! You make me laugh
There ain't no pomp in this small strafe
I'm bombing hell from a local Khan
To keep the Peace of Waziristan!"

"Oh smart Brisfit! Oh smart Brisfit!
What are you doing in fighting kit?"

"I'm praying hard to avoid a 'konk'
On offensive patrol from a sink called Tonk
Down the gorges and up Splitoi
Sniped to blazes but, Attaboy!
They called it war on the banks of the Marne
But bless you! it's Peace in Waziristan!"

"If they ask me, what shall I say
To the folks at home, back England way?"

"Don't you worry — there's naught to tell
'Cept work and fly and bomb like hell —
With hills above and hills below
And rocks to pile where the hills won't go —
Nice soft sitting for those who crash
But 'War' you call it? Don't talk trash
War's a rumour — war's a yarn
This is the Peace of Waziristan'

R. H. Peel

The Desert Mail

With few landing grounds, and fewer navigational aids, R.A.F. crews pioneered the air mail routes that others would later follow with far less risk.

Clean cut against the first faint flush of dawn,
  Their silver planes outstretched to catch the sun,
Hastening to meet the Day as yet unborn,
  Faint upon the earth their engines muted hum.
Below the Desert lies in shadow dim,
  A vast, inverted bowl of yellow sand,
The distant hills, eternal guardians grim,
  Flanking the entrance to a barren land.

For His Majesty's Mails are travelling East,
  (Mark the Track as it winds below)
His Majesty's Mails are travelling East,
  (Six hundred weary miles to go!)

The ashes of a fire — lit all in vain—
  A Thing that breathed and lived but yesterday,
The charred and blackened wreckage of a 'plane,
  Are all that mark the Man Who Lost his Way.
An error of a minute; a side-slip in a cloud;
  He failed to see the Track he thought he knew,
The endless days of waiting — by fear and hunger cowed—
  Ere the jackals took the meat that was their due!

For His Majesty's Mails are travelling East,
  (The Track is dim in the sand below.)
His Majesty's Mails are travelling East.
  (Only two hundred miles to go!)

In the bitter cold of Winter, when the sullen engines fret,
  And the leaden sky above them bids them stay,
In the storm or in the sunshine; in the dry or in the wet,
  The Air Mail passes swiftly on its way.
In the hottest days of Summer, when the water-holes are
  dry,
  And the Desert's full of things that are not there,
The gaunt and weary jackal sees the shadows passing by
  Of the Mail 'planes as they hurry through the air.

For His Majesty's Mails are travelling East.
  (The Arrow is pointing the way to go.)
His Majesty's Mails are travelling East.
  (Those are the Bitumen Pools below!)

We have placed at your disposal all the arts we learnt in War,
  And for ninepence you can purchase, if you're wise,
The same efficient service of the Man who Yesterday,
  Chased the black-crossed Birds of War from out your
  skies,
The letters that they carry from Cairo to the East,
  Bear little slips of paper, coloured blue,
And the loss of crew and pilot doesn't matter in the least,
  If the Mail Bags see the Desert journey through!

For His Majesty's Mails are travelling East.
  (The Track is lost but the way we know.)
His Majesty's Mails are travelling East.
  (Baghdad City to port below!)

Robert Jope Slade

No. 60's D.H.10's

In the early 1920s No. 60 Squadron R.A.F. were equipped with D.H.10's for their operations in the North-West Frontier Province of India. It would appear that the D.H.10 was no better than the D.H.9!

We've had these 'buses about a year,
At first in Blighty and then out here,
Yet our pilots aren't afraid
To take them on a joyride
Or on a bombing raid.
Other squadrons say they're quite unsafe
And so they stick to D.H.9's
But 60 Squadron laugh at them
As they set out for the Afghan lines,
And when one engine cuts right out
They land at the nearest 'drome and shout —

There are Camels, there are Pups, there are S.E.5's
And millionaires can buy a Handley Page,
There are Kangaroos, B.E.2's and the
Nieuport Nighthawk is now the rage.
Most every day we have a crash or two,
That's why we are so short of men;
So if you want to take a trip to Heaven quick
You've only got to fly a D.H.10.

That Old-Fashioned Avro of Mine

Sung to the tune of "That Old Fashioned Mother of Mine", the words vary according to which was your favourite aircraft. This version (Avro 504K) was a Flying Training School adaptation of the original.

There are fellows who swear at machines in the air,
At mechanics who rig them and don't seem to care,
But there's a machine which is oily and slow,
And it's locked in the heart of a tree that I know.

Just an old-fashioned Avro with old-fashioned ways
And a kick that says "Back-fire" to you,
An old Mono engine that konks out and stays
When the toil of a long flight is through,
Though the pressure will drop and it loses its prop
And the pilot's inclined to resign,
I'll rejoice till I die — that I learned how to fly
On that old-fashioned Avro of mine.

There are finer machines with much better wind-screens
And whose pilots don't know what a dud engine means
But my good old Avro can loop, roll or spin
There isn't a field that I can't put her in.

Just an old-fashioned Avro, etc.

Sky Fever

A strong dose of flying is the only known cure for Sky Fever. In trembling anticipation you go to your airfield; but no, the fickle weather mocks you! Never mind there's always tomorrow....or the day after?

I must go up in the air again, in the glorious
air and the sky,
And all I ask is a kind C.O. and a tolerant C.F.I.
A calm day, a cloudless sky, and the taught wires
humming,
And a heat haze over green grass, and the engine
sweetly running.

I must go up in the air again. O speak to the C.F.I.
He's a hard man, and a mean man, that would keep us
away from the sky.
And the sole excuse is a showery day, with the grey
clouds flying.
Or a ground mist over the aerodrome, the use of the
air denying.

I must go up in the air again. But I see a black
cone high,
And if not that, not quite so bad, the dual cone I spy.
But the clouds clear, and the sun shines, and the mist
blows off the clover,
It's a grand day and a clear sky — when the flying
period's over.

Flt/Cdt. P. R. Hatfield,
R.A.F. College Cranwell

Fall in, and Fly

Almost too late (as usual) the politicians agreed to re-build the R.A.F. This flag-waving song was written to encourage young men to join: they need not have bothered — this country has never suffered from a shortage of aircrew volunteers!

Take the air, leave every blessed care
Like the flying boys do,
Seek your fun much nearer the sun
Climb right into the blue,
— Why don't you —
Leave the crowds, get up among the clouds
Where the sun shines on high,
You can be there if you try,
Fall in, and fly.

The Pilot's 23rd Psalm

An excellent example of teaching by the "humorous" method. The reader is more likely to remember these words of wisdom and, in remembering, become a safer (better) pilot.

1. As the telephone operator who giveth wrong numbers so is he who extolleth his exploits in the air.

2. He shall enlarge upon the dangers of his adventures, but in my sleeve shall be heard the tinkling of silvery laughter.

3. Let not thy familiarity with aeroplanes breed contempt, lest thou become exceedingly careless at a time when great care is necessary to thy well-being.

4. My son, obey the law and observe prudence. Spin thou not lower than 1500 cubits nor stunt above thine own domicile. For the hand of the law is heavy and reacheth far and wide throughout the land.

5. Incur not the wrath of thy Commander by breaking the rules; for he who maketh right-hand circuits shall be cast out into utter darkness.

6. Let not thy prowess in the air persuade thee that others cannot do even as thou doest; for he that showeth off in public places is an abomination unto his fellow pilots.

7. More praiseworthy is he who can touch tail-skid and wheels to earth at one time, than he who loopeth and rolleth till some damsel stares in amazement at his daring.

8. He who breaketh an undercarriage in a forced landing may, in time, be forgiven, but he who taxieth into another aircraft shall be despised forever.

9. Beware the man who taketh off without looking behind him, for there is no health in him verily, I say unto you, his days are numbered.

10. Clever men take the reproofs of their instructors in the same wise, one like unto another: with witty jest, confessing their dumbness and regarding themselves with humour. Yet they try again, profiting by his wise counsel and taking not offence at aught that has been said.

11. As a postage stamp which lacketh glue, so are the words of caution to a fool; they stick not, going in one ear and out the other, for there is nothing between to stop them.

12. My son, hearken unto my teaching and forsake not the laws of prudence, for the reckless shall not inhabit the earth for long.

13. Hear instruction and be wise, and refuse it not; thus wilt thou fly safely; length of days and a life of peace shall be added unto thee.

Captain J. D. Olive

"Old Bus"

Australia's hero, one of the greatest pilots of all time, Sir Charles Kingsford Smith ("Smithy") K.B.E., M.C., A.F.C., wrote this poem in farewell to his record-breaking aircraft Southern Cross, which is now fittingly preserved at Brisbane Airport, Australia.

Old faithful friend — a long adieu!
These are poor words with which to tell
Of all my pride, my joy in you.
True to the end you served me well.

I pity those who cannot see
That heart and soul are housed within
This thing of steel and wood — to me
You live in every bolt and pin.

And so, my staunch and steadfast steed,
Your deep and mighty voice must cease.
Faithful to death. If God will heed
My prayer, dear pal, you'll rest in peace.

Charles Kingsford Smith

The Alderman Looks Up and Back

"The boast of heraldry, the pomp of power" fade away as this dignitary remembers his truly golden days when he wore his "wings".

My Aldermanic couch is old,
  And I am fifty, fat and proud;
But once I looped and spun and rolled
  With lads like you above the cloud.

Our stalling speed was eighty then,
  And England looked like stalling too,
But England finds her Englishmen
  To see the hour of danger through.

My Aldermanic robes are new
  And yet I feel but half as proud
As when I wore my Air Force blue,
  And climbed above a cirrus cloud.

Leonard Taylor

WINGS OF WAR, 1939-1945

And so it came to pass that, on 3rd September 1939, Britain was once again at war with Germany; a Germany that had been surreptitiously re-building its air force over the years until it had become the strongest in the world. Despite many warnings of this build-up by both Intelligence and eye-witness reports, Britain had been slow to react and it was only in the last few years prior to the outbreak of hostilities that an expansion of the R.A.F. took place — but too much time had been lost. There were not enough fighters for both attack and defence; not enough bombers to land telling punches; not enough coastal aircraft to give adequate protection to the convoys and, even if there had have been, there were not enough training schools to turn out the required numbers of aircrews.

However, the skies were not entirely overcast. The R.A.F., though small in numbers, was of a high quality; inventors and designers were now free to go ahead with their creations, and that old intangible — patriotism — was again sweeping through the British Empire. There was no shortage of aircrew volunteers, only, as stated, the means to train them. At this point a tribute must be paid to those members of the ground staff who, without extra rank (or brevets), helped to fill the gap, the Armourers, Flight Mechanics and Wireless Operators who volunteered to fly. These were the Supernumaries, the unsung heroes of operational flying.

The air war began in earnest on 10 May 1940 when the shadows of the *Luftwaffe's* wings raced across Holland, Belgium and France. The Hurricanes, Blenheims and (shades of the B.E.2C) the inadequate Battles of the R.A.F.

fought back but, outnumbered and continually losing their airfields to the rapidly advancing German army, they were fighting a losing battle and by mid July the were back in England — or what was left of them were. Then came the Battle of Britain. The two old adversaries severely punished each other in the aerial arena over southern England. It was a very close contest; close because of Britain's unpreparedness, close because of a shortage of pilots, aircraft, airfields, of almost everything except courage. Tragically, history was repeating itself in that young pilots with very few hours on Spitfires and Hurricanes were thrown into the greatest aerial battle of all time. The painful lesson of 1917 had been forgotten.

The sorry story continued: Greece, Crete, the Western Desert, and in Malta where, initially, a few Gladiators faced the Italian Air Force and, not least, in the Far East where Buffalo fought Zero in a one-sided contest while the obsolete Vildebeest made its heroic torpedo attacks when it should have been relegated long since to a training role at best. And all through the darkest hours of 1940, 1941 and the early part of 1942 the land-based airmen were aided, and very much abetted, by their nautical comrades of the Fleet Air Arm who hit the enemy hard and often in their old "Stringbags".

However, the depths had been plumbed and the skies grew lighter as 1942 progressed. The Empire Air Training Scheme, started in 1940, was turning out a steady stream of aircrews. The aircraft and ammunition factories, protected now by a formidable night-fighter defence, were at full blast. Bomber Command was hitting German production by night and the U.S.A.A.F. had begun its daylight raids. It was air supremacy that helped the Army to push the enemy from the Western Desert and enabled battered Malta once again to become a very prickly thorn in the side of the Axis powers.

From then on Allied air power climbed steadily onwards and upwards; co-operation with the land and sea forces was improving all the time. In 1943 the invasions of Sicily and Italy were accomplished with little intervention from the hard-pressed *Luftwaffe*. The pressure increased by day and by night; on industry, communications, shipping, on the hated U-boat until, in June 1944, came retribution in the shape of the invasion of France: a vast sea armada protected by the now mighty wings of allied air supremacy. In the Far East, too, the tide had turned, flowing towards ultimate victory for the avenging Allies.

In the pursuit of victory it is natural to look only forward, and it was not until after that goal had been achieved that people looked back, perhaps with a quickening of the pulse, to those dark early days of the war and realised how dangerously close to defeat they had been. It was only then that one could begin to realise the true values of the battles of Britain and Malta in particular, and wonder at the determination and selfless courage of those who had fought them — the men who had started the Allies on the long climb back.

In terms of numbers of men, aircraft and areas of operation there is no comparison between the two air wars, but the men who flew in them are utterly comparable: they knew the same joys and fears that go hand in hand in their chosen profession — chosen because they were all volunteers — they shared the same special comradeship of those who fly...they shared the same war-torn skies.

"We Don't Want to Join The Air Force"

The origin of this ditty is lost in the smokey haze of a thousand Messes and bars, but certainly it was sung more frequently in the Second World War. Some words (indicated by parentheses) vary according to the mood of the singer!

We don't want to join the Air Force,
We don't want to go to war;
We'd sooner hang around
Piccadilly Underground,
Living on the earnings of a high-born lady.
'Don't want bullets in our (rudder)
'Don't want our (tailplane) shot away;
We'd rather stay in England
Merry, merry, England
(Boozing) the rest of our lives away!

A Young English Airman

The soldier, by the evidence of his own eyes, thought that the R.A.F. had deserted him at Dunkirk. In fact, the R.A.F., by breaking up large formations en route to the beaches, prevented a massacre of our troops.

O smiling, sun-burned youth who rode the sky
Like to the sparrow-hawk or summer swift,
And watched your shadow flitting on the drift
Far underneath you as you hurried by.

Six months ago to-day you put off bird
To gleam as ion in a nation's will,
To save the ruined friends and then lie still,
Spring never to be touched by summer's word.

Often unseen by those you helped to save
You rode the air above that foreign dune
And died like the unutterably brave
That so your friends might see the English June.

Haply, in some sharp instant in mid-sky,
When you, at the bird's summit, took the lunge
Of the foe's bitterness that made you die,
And the bright bird declined into her plunge,

You, from the Heaven, saw, in English chalk
White, about Dover, some familiar track,
That feet of yours would never again walk
Since you were killed and never coming back,

Yet knew, that your young life, as price paid over
Let thousands live to tread that track to Dover.

John Masefield

Passing of a Hurricane

This salute to the Hawker Hurricane catches the spirit that prevailed in that now-legendary time — "Our Finest Hour"

As I walked down by Lewis Lane
  To buy a roasting duck
There passed a broken Hurricane
  Dismembered on a truck

Her wings lay folded at her side,
  A blackened, tattered pall,
And gaping bullet-holes supplied
  The context of her fall.

The canvas discs which normally
  Screen the eight gun-vents' blast
Were shot away — brave proof that she
  Fell firing to the last.

She went, and as I sort my roast
  I thanked her for the day
When high above the Kentish coast
  She dived into the fray

And quite alone, no friends to see
  Fought twenty Messerschmitts
Who, having scored but one to three,
  Repented of their blitz

Then sudden, as I stopped and stood,
  A roar came deep and strong —
A squadron of her sisterhood
  Throating their battlesong.

"Ariel"

War

One of the Few, Nigel Weir was awarded the D.F.C. during the Battle of Britain. Shot down and killed in November, 1940, he died knowing that the Battle had been won.

When the bloom is off the garden,
and I'm fighting in the sky,
when the lawns and flower beds harden,
and when weak birds starve and die,
and death-roll will grow longer,
eyes will be moist and red;
and the more I kill, the longer
shall I miss friends who are dead.

F/O Nigel Weir,
D.F.C., R.A.F.

Sonnet to a Windsock

Pilots often give the windsock the briefest of glances: not so the Chaplain of R.A.F. Biggin Hill in 1940 who took a very long look at this faithful, and truthful, friend of the flier.

Brave canvas on a thousand breezes borne,
Now on some scrapheap destined to be thrown,
By bullets riddled, and bomb splinters torn,
These fateful months you faithfully have flown,
For bloodshot eyes within the circuit flying,
The wind's own eye precisely you have found; —
Young men — and some are hurt and some are dying, —
At ninety knots they glide from air to ground.
Towards you my vizored friends, with one last glance,
Unleashed their Merlins — took off into cloud,
James fell in flames and Christopher in France,
For Peter and for Simon sea was shroud.
Shall 'danger-money' workmen end your year?
'Give it me please!' Young voices fill my ear.

W. D. O'Hanlon

The Flying Instructor's Lament

His experience too valuable to be risked on operations, the frustrated instructor carried on with his all-important task, finding consolation in the achievements of his former pupils.

'What did you do in the war, Daddy?
How did you help us to win?'
'Circuits and bumps and turns, laddy,
And how to get out of a spin'

Woe and alack and misery me! I trundle round in the sky,
And instead of machine-gunning Nazis I'm teaching young hopefuls to fly;
Thus is my service rewarded, my years of experience paid,
Never a Hun have I followed right down nor ever gone out on a raid.

They don't even let us go crazy, we have to be safe and sedate,
So it's nix on inverted approaches, they stir up the C.F.I.'s hate.
For it's oh! such a naughty example, and what will the A.O.C. think!
But we never get posted to fighters — we just get a spell on the Link.

So it's circuits and bumps from morning till noon,
and instrument-flying till tea.
'Hold her off, give her bank, put your undercart
down, you're skidding, you're slipping'—that's me.
And as soon as you've finished with one course, like
a flash up another one bobs,
And there's four more to show round the cockpit and
four more to try out the knobs.

But sometimes we read in the papers of the deeds that
old pupils have done,
And we're proud to have seen their beginnings and
shown them the way to the sun;
So if you find the money and turn out the planes
we'll give all we know to the men
Till they cluster the sky with their triumphs and
burn out the beast from his den.

"If I Only Had Wings"

The refrain of this popular song of the 1940s tells of an "Erks" dream of wings. Alas, for the majority of the dreamers, the dream never came true.

If I only had wings!
Oh, what a difference it would make to things.
All day long I'd be in the sky,
Up on high,
Talking to the birdies as they passed me by.
How the fellows would stare,
To see me roaring past them thro' the air,
Never tiring of the thrill it brings,
If I only had wings!
I'd be so fearless and bold
That when the stories of my deeds were told,
You'd see my picture in the papers,
And they would proudly say
"The R.A.F. and me we had another good day"
If I only had wings!
One little pair of those elusive things
You would never hear me complain again —
If I only had wings!
If I only had wings!

S. Collins & R. Aldrich

Security

As an R.A.F. Intelligence Officer no one was more fully aware than this poet of the need for the strictest security prior to operations.

Empty your pockets, Tom, Dick and Harry,
Strip your identity; leave it behind.
Lawyer, garage-hand, grocer, don't tarry
With your own country, your own kind.

Leave all your letters. Suburb and township,
Green fen and grocery, slipway and bay,
Hot spring and prairie, smoke stack and coal tip,
Leave in our keeping while you're away.

Tom, Dick, and Harry, plain names and numbers,
Pilot, observer, and gunner depart.
Their personal litter only encumbers
Somebody's head, somebody's heart.

John Pudney

For Johnny

This poem, from the film The Way to the Stars, *underline the poet's personal feelings for the aircres whose return he awaited...sometimes in vain...*

Do not despair
For Johnny-head-in-air;
He sleeps as sound
As Johnny underground.

Fetch out no shroud
For Johnny-in-the-cloud;
And keep your tears
For him in after years.

Better by far
For Johnny the bright star,
To keep your head,
And see his children fed.

John Pudney

"Operations Calling!"

Pilot Officer Bourne, R.A.F.V.R., was shot down and killed on 5th September 1941. Among his poems was this one which recalls the urgency of a "Scramble".

"Clearing Black Section
Patrol Bass Rock,"
Leaps heart; after shock
Action comes stumbling;
Snatch your helmet;
Then run smoothly, to the grumbling
Of a dozing Merlin heating
Supercharged air,
You are there
by "Z"

Down hard on the behind
The parachute; you are blind
With your oxygen snout
But click, click, click, click, you feel
and the harness is fixed.
Round the wing
And "Out of the cockpit, you,"
Clamber the rung
And the wing as if a wasp had stung
You, hop and jump into the cockpit,
Split second to spike
The Sutton harness holes,
One, two, three, four,
Thrust with your
Hand to the throttle open.......

"Operations" called and spoken.

P/O David Bourne.

High Flight

Considered by many airmen to be a classic, this beautiful poem was written by a nineteen year old R.C.A.F. pilot, who was killed in action on 11th December 1941.

Oh, I have slipped the surly bonds of Earth
And danced the skies on laughter-silvered wings;
Sunward I've climbed and joined the tumbling mirth
Of sun-split clouds — and done a hundred things
You have not dreamed of — wheeled and soared and swung
High in the sunlit silence; hovering there,
I've chased the shouting wind along, and flung
My eager craft through footless halls of air.

Up, up the long, delirious burning blue
I've topped the wind-swept heights with easy grace
Where never lark, or even eagle ever flew —
And, while with silent lifting mind I've trod
The high untrespassed sanctity of space,
Put out my hand and touched the face of God.

John Gillespie Magee, Jr.

Epilogue

Outnumbered and without respite, a few R.A.F. squadrons fought to the bitter end in the skies above Greece. Their endeavours were truly Homeric.

The solemn march of these immortal few
Is beating in the skies;
From silent ranks there gleams the steadfast light
Of triumph in their eyes;
They know the ecstacy of battle's thrill,
And victory's finest prize.

Though they were few, too few, who fought in Greece
They waged a constant fight;
A new mythology of glorious deeds
Their mountain tombstones write;
So tell their lasting honour to the world,
And keep their torch alight.

James Gordon

When A Beau Goes In

In the grim accounting of war the loss of one Beaufighter is but a small debit, but to those who knew the crew the loss is incalculable.

When a Beau goes in,
Into the drink,
It makes you think,
Because, you see, they always sink
But nobody says 'Poor lad'
Or goes about looking sad
Because, you see, it's war,
It's the unalterable law.

Although it's perfectly certain
The pilot's gone for a Burton
And the observer too
Its nothing to do with you
And if they both should go
To a land where falls no rain no hail
  nor driven snow —
Here, there or anywhere,
Do you suppose they care?

You shouldn't cry
Or say a prayer or sigh,
In the cold sea, in the dark,
It isn't a lark
But it isn't Original Sin —
It's just a Beau going in.

Gavin Ewart

The Pilots' Paradise

A nice thought this, an Elysian airfield. Sceptics may scoff but there is only one person who really knows...and He won't tell mere mortals.

High above Betelgeuse, they say,
  Beyond Orion's questing eyes,
Ten million star-strewn years away
  There hangs a pilots' paradise.

Thither when airmen's bodies fall
  Their spirits climb on eager wing
To greet old comrades and recall
  Old days of earthward sojourning.

They talk of 'flak', intruders, beams,
  Of dummy runs and how to weave,
Sorties and strikes, and tales like dreams
  Which none but airmen would believe.

From aerodromes like cloth of green
  Mid cloudless skies for ever blue
They sport themselves; and each machine
  Is every morning bright and new.

And every pilot when he lands
  Three-pointed sweeps the glossy lawn;
With young keen eye and strong young hands
  He climbs to meet each glowing dawn.

What dawns are those, what noonday sun
  From which no enemies descend,
What flights when duty here is done
  To enter at your log-book's end!

O.C.C.

"Lie in the Dark and Listen"

In his tribute this man of many talents shows his very real understanding of the drama enacted nightly by the aircrews of Bomber Command.

Lie in the dark and listen
It's clear tonight so they're flying high,
Hundreds of them, thousands perhaps,
Riding the icy, moonlight sky,
Men, machinery, bombs and maps,
Altimeters and guns and charts,
Coffee, sandwiches, fleece-lined boots,
Bones and muscles and minds and hearts
English saplings with English roots
Deep in the earth they've left below.
Lie in the dark and let them go;
Lie in the dark and listen.

Noel Coward

Swordfish

The grand old "Stringbag" was obsolescent before the War, yet served throughout in many theatres. Few aircraft could equal her battle honours.

Between a cloud and a cloud
I saw you glide
in that last light, lees of the cup of day,
Your good old "Peggy" bumbling away:
the sky, and the night, and the sea beneath you,
wide and lonely, three infinities of grey.

But you had purpose, Swordfish. You were going
about your business at that steady amble
which seems so comic to those who have not seen
your shaking, snaking path when you are throwing
yourself about the sky, shell-bursts between each bank,
or out-turning a fighter in the gamble
for hitting-space,
you fraud of a Stringbag, you.

What can you do with a Stringbag?
What can't you do
you can aerobat; you can stand her on her tail;
go into a vertical dive — and pull out sweetly
(you won't find the Stringbag doing a high-speed stall).
You can take her up in any weather at all
that can be flown in,
you can trust her completely
even if visibility's next to nil,
or you have to land in a mid-Atlantic gale.
Whatever the jobs you give her, she will not fail -
if there are kills to be made she'll be in at the kill.
Bombing? She carries more than a Blenheim does -

and watch her spot for the guns of the Battle Fleet!
She'll torpedo a cruiser as soon as she gets the buzz,
and (you ask Doenitz) the U-boats are her meat.

Oh, they spoil you for other aircraft for good, do Sword-
fishes —
they've always looked obsolescent, they've never been
obsolete;
they give a fellow the feeling of confidence and ease
like a seasoned pipe, or a dog you've trained, or old shoes
kind to the feet.
For crews have learned to trust them who have had time to
learn:
in long lone hours of night flight when the sky is a dry-point
plate
as in the infinite instant of the first evasive turn
after the fish strikes water, and they open up on the crate.

Well. They've stopped producing Stringbags. And doubt-
less They know best.
I'll fly the kites they give me — and think of my earliest love.
They're grand are the Barracudas, and the Seafires and the
rest,
but — I know what the Palmist meant, now,
when he sighed for the wings of a dove.
And after the war is over, when the Brave New World
appears,
with planes to suit all pockets, and a seat in a sky-train's
cheap,
if I cannot purchase a Stringbag to solace my latter years —
as, once, men took to a bathchair, perhaps I'll take to a Jeep.

R. C. Scriven

An Ode to the U-Boats (269's Hymn of Hate)

The aircrews of B Flight, No. 269 Squadron, wrote this poem which leaves no room for doubt about their "avowed intent" to relentlessly hunt down and destroy the U-Boats.

O, slinky, slimy, slithering snake,
You make poor trawlers quiver and quake,
  But following your elusive feather
  In every kind of dirty weather,
In rain or hail, snow or fine
Come those who'll catch you — 269.

You hide beneath the waters green,
But we will find you, submarine.
  Although you in our channels lurk
  To try to do your dirty work,
That death-portending screaming whine
Means you've been seen by 269.

Your conning tower, that glorious sight
Comes into view just on the right.
  The bombs are live, the eye is keen
  Crash-dive you cowardly submarine,
This bomb will break your slinky spine —
A job well done by — 269.

Now, submarine, take this to heart,
Ere your next raid is due to start,
  Your chance is NIL; the odds too great;
  So shoot yourself; it's not too late.
If you're not blown up by a mine
You sure will be by 269.

The Eagle Squadrons

They came from the U.S.A. to a war that was not of their making. They became Nos. 71, 121 and 133 Squadrons, R.A.F., but to the free world they were better known as the American "Eagles".

Lord, hold them in thy mighty hand
Above the ocean and the land
Like wings of Eagles mounting high
Along the pathways of the sky.

Immortal is the name they bear
And high the honour that they share.
Until a thousand years have rolled,
Their deeds of valour shall be told.

In dark of night and light of day
God speed and bless them on their way
And homeward safely guide each one
With glory gained and duty done.

In the Local

The "couldn't-care-less" attitude of the off-duty fighter pilots was a cover for their true feelings, camouflaging the day-to-day tensions.

You see them in the "Local" anywhere
  In town or country near a fighter station
In flying boots and scarves — their ruffled hair
  Like schoolboys out for a jolly celebration:
Eight in a car for four had raced along
  And miracles were wrought to bring them here.
To pass an hour with banter, darts and song
  And drink a pint or two of English beer,
And talk of "binds" and "dims" with lots of natter
  Of "ropey jobs" and "wizard types" and "gen"
Amid much laughter glasses chink and clatter.
  Deep underneath was hid the real men,
Who saw their comrades fall out of the skies,
  And knew too well the look in dead men's eyes.

W. A. G. Kemp

Airmen From Overseas

Kiwis, Aussies, Springboks, Canucks, and many others; they could have waited, enjoyed the peace of their own lands for a little longer — but they did not.

Who are these that come from the ends of the oceans,
Coming as the swallows come out of the South
In the glory of Spring? They are come among us
With purpose in the eyes, with a smile on the mouth.

These are they who have left the familiar faces,
Sights, sounds and scents of familiar land,
Taking no care for security promised aforetime,
Sweetness of home and the future hope had planned.

A lode-star has drawn them; Britain, standing alone
Clear in the darkness, not to be overcome,
Though the huge masses of hate are hurled against her,
Wherever the spirit of freedom breathes, is Home

Soon they are joined with incomparable comrades,
Britain's flower and Britain's pride,
Against all odds, despising the boastful Terror,
On joyous wings in the ways of the wind they ride.

From afar they battle for our ancient island,
Soaring and pouncing, masters of the skies.
They are heard in the night by lands betrayed and captive.
And a throbbing of hope to their thunder-throb replies.

To dare incredible things, from the ends of ocean
They are coming and coming, over the perilous seas,
How shall we hail them? Truly there are no words
And no song worthy of these.

Laurence Binyon

Empty Stringbag on the Safi Strip

After months of gruelling night operations from battered Malta, No. 830 Squadron, R.N., almost ceased to exist, which prompted one of their number to write new lyrics to the song "Empty Saddles in the Old Corral".

Empty Stringbag on the Safi Strip
Why don't you fly tonight?
Is there shrapnel in your mainplanes,
Are your pistons slightly teased,
Have you got a bombhole in your pen?

Empty Stringbag on the Safi Strip,
Why don't you fly tonight?
Did the Riggers all forsake you,
Have they hidden underground,
Are they waiting for a hundred plus?

Empty tanks bunged up with rust.
Why don't you leak tonight?
Lousy brakes, smothered in dust,
Why don't you squeak tonight?

Empty Stringbag on the Safi Strip,
My tears would be dry tonight,
If you'd only totter skywards,
With your Peggy grinding hard,
Empty Stringbag on the Safi Strip.

A member of No. 830 Sqdn. R.N.

Official Song of the Army Air Forces

On 17th August 1942, American bombers flew their first mission to Rouen. Comparatively few "ships" took part — they were later to be followed by armadas. This was — and still is — the U.S.A.A.F's song.

Off we go into the wild blue yonder,
Climbing high into the sun;
Here they come, zooming to meet our thunder,
At 'em boys, give 'er the gun!
(Give 'er the gun now!)
Down we dive, spouting out flame from under,
Up again with one hell-uv-a roar!
We live in fame or go down in flame,
Nothing'll stop the Army Air Corps!

Chorus: Here's a toast to the host of those who
love the vastness of the sky,
To a friend we send a message of his
brother men who fly.
We drink to those who gave their all of old,
Then down we roar to score the rainbow's
pot of gold.
A toast to the host of men we boast, the
Army Air Corps!

Minds of men fashioned a crate of thunder,
Set it high into the blue;
Hands of men blasted the world asunder;
How they lived God only knew!
(God only knew then)
Souls of men dreaming of skies to conquer
Gave us wings, ever to soar!
With scouts before and bombers galore,
Nothing'll stop the Army Air Corps!

Chorus: Here's a toast, etc.

Off we go into the wild sky yonder.
Keep the wings level and true;
If you'd live to be a grey-haired wonder
Keep the nose out of the blue!
(Out of the blue boy!)
Flying men, guarding the nation's border,
We'll be there, followed by more!
In echelon we carry on,
Nothing'll stop the Army Air Corps!

Chorus: Here's a toast, etc.

Robert Crawford

Epitaph for F/Lt Jean "Peiker" Offenberg, D.F.C.

This popular Belgian "ace" typified the spirit of the Free Belgian airmen who refused to surrender and carried on the fight alongside the R.A.F.

Here, in the corner of an English shire,
Far from the homeland that he fought to save,
A Belgian pilot sleeps, who dying gave
His all, for all of England to admire.

Here was a warrior of the lonely sky,
Modest and brave, outstanding of his race,
Who winged the outer air with swallow's grace —
To us it hardly seemed that he could die.

And many friends who loved him, and who live,
Live thanks to him — his was the magic touch
That plucked them from the death he scorned so much,
And like a shepherd homed them. Do not grieve
If you should pass this way in after years —
His was a life that shone too bright for tears.

Frank Ziegler

Fulmar II

The Fleet Air Arm too disliked certain aircraft, and the aircrews of H.M.S. Victorious concocted this criticism of the Fulmar Mk II, which they sang to the old Cockney tune of "Any Old Iron"

Any old iron, any old iron,
Any, any, any, old iron;
Talk about a treat,
Chasing round the Fleet
Any old Eyetie or Hun you meet

Weighs six ton
No rear gun
Damn all to rely on!

You know what you can do
With your Fulmar Two
Old iron, old iron.

The Benghazi Mail Run

In the Desert War the aircrews of No. 70 Squadron, R.A.F. bombed the port of Benghazi so regularly that it became, for them, a "mail run". They sang their song to the tune of "My Darling Clementine". The numbers 60 and 09 denote Landing Grounds.

Take off for the Western Desert,
  Fuka, 60 or 09,
Same old Wimpey, same old target,
  Same old aircrew, same old time.

Chorus: Seventy Squadron, Seventy Squadron,
    Though we say it with a sigh,
    Must we do this ruddy Mail Run
    Every night until we die?

Navigator have you lost us?
  Come up here and have a look,
Someone's shot our starboard wing off,
  That's alright then that's Tobruk.

Chorus: Seventy Squadron, etc.

Forty Wimpeys on the target,
  Two were ditched down in the drink,
Then three others crashed on landing,
  Bloomin' hell, it makes you think.

Chorus: Seventy Squadron, etc.

Stooging round the Western Desert,
  With the gravy running low,
How I wish I could see Fuka,
  Through the sandstorm down below.

Chorus: Seventy Squadron, etc.

First it's Derna, then it's Barce,
  Even the I.O. isn't sure —
They've changed the bomb load twice already,
  It's a proper Cookies Tour.

Chorus: Seventy Squadron, etc.

All this flapping cannot fool us,
  We know just where we'll have to be,
Rumour's heard of a new target,
  But after all it's just B.G.

Chorus: Seventy Squadron, etc.

To Benghazi is the slogan,
  We'll take the load right through once more,
So start your engines, let's get cracking,
  The mail runs going as before.

Chorus: Seventy Squadron, etc.

'Telligence tells us from his photos
  We never hit a single flea,
Sees no bomb holes in the rooftops
  Only craters in the sea.

Chorus: Seventy Squadron, etc.

He asks us if we're "sure we pranged?"
  Must have been some other spot
Suggests we bombed a dummy target,
  Never heard such utter clot!

Chorus: Seventy Squadron, etc.

Try to get your tour of ops. in
  Without your aircraft being hit,
If you do you'll go to Blighty,
  If you don't you're in the pit.

Chorus: Seventy Squadron, etc.

Oh to be in Piccadilly
  Selling matches by the score!
Though we'd feel a little chilly,
  There'd be no mail run any more.

Chorus: Seventy Squadron, etc.

Richard Hillary

Fighter "ace", "Guinea-pig" and author of The Last Enemy, Richard Hillary returned to flying after recovering from severe burns sustained in the Battle of Britain, but was killed whilst re-training on night fighters.

Summon the buglers, Captain of the Guard!
  For, young in years, but in achievement old,
  From that high air whose glorious tale he told,
He comes, a veteran in battle scarred.

The noonday terror he had faced and fought —
  O gallant few to whom our all was owed! —
  And, stricken down, deemed life again bestowed
For one sole end; and, even as he wrought

With splendid pen, craved but the one reward
  To stay the pestilence that flies by night,
  Met the last enemy, and won that fight.
Summon the buglers, Captain of the Guard!

C. A. A.

The Flying-Weather Seer

The men and women of the Air Transport Auxiliary released R.A.F. pilots from thousands of hours of ferrying duties. At the end of the war there were over six hundred A.T.A. fliers...during the war 143 lost their lives.

The taxi Anson's piled with flying kit,
Each ferry pilot cons his morning chit,
When from the weather office comes the cry
That to the west black clouds bestride the sky.
Then out "Met's" head is thrust from windows wide
This dark portent to ponder or deride;
'Tis dull, 'tis dark, the cloud's precipitating,
No weather this for us to aviate in!
But one more bold by far than all the rest
Out to the runway taxis, gazes west,
Raises an eyebrow, casts his eyes about,
Wriggles his corns, his shoulder blades, his snout.
Instinct at work — will it be wet or fine?
What does this Flying-Weather seer divine?
He turns about and trundles back to "Met"
To tell them that it really will be wet.

Anon. A.T.A. Pilot

Unidentified

Unarmed, the Photo-Recce pilots flew very high — or very low. Hazards enough without the Gremlins who, some say, did not exist...or did they?

This is the tale of the Gremlins
  Told by the P.R.U.
At Benson and Wick and St. Eval —
  And believe me, you slobs, it's true.

When you're seven miles up in the heavens,
  (That's a hell of a lonely spot)
And it's fifty degrees below zero
  Which isn't exactly hot.

When you're frozen blue like your Spitfire
  And you're scared a mosquito pink,
When you're thousands of miles from nowhere
  And there's nothing below but the drink—

It's then that you will see the Gremlins,
  Green and gamboge and gold,
Male and female and neuter,
  Gremlins both young and old.

It's no good trying to dodge them,
  The lesson you learnt on the link
Won't help you evade a Gremlin
  Though you boost and you dive and you jink.

White ones will wiggle your wingtips,
  Male ones will muddle your maps,
Green ones will guzzle your Glycol,
  Females will flutter your flaps.

Pink ones will perch on your perspex,
  And dance pirouettes on your prop;
There's a spherical middle-aged Gremlin
  Who'll spin on your stick like a top.

They'll freeze up your camera shutters,
  They'll bite through your aileron wires,
They'll bend and they'll break and they'll batter,
  They'll insert toasting forks in your tyres.

That is the tale of the Gremlins,
  Told by the P.R.U.,
(P)retty (R)uddy (U)nlikely to many,
  But fact, none the less, to the few.

Anon P.R.U. Pilot

Sons of the Lords of the Air

During the war over 100,000 cadets of the Air Training Corps joined the R.A.F. for both air and ground duties. Of these many won decorations — one the V.C. — and many others failed to return. This was the Corp's song — they meant every word.

Gentlemen, the Air Force; this will be our toast,
To the silver wings that saved the things
Our Country loves the most.
Gentlemen, remember, we must do the same,
We the 'aces' of tomorrow proudly take their name.

We're the Sons of the Lords of the Air —
We're the A.T.C.,
For a place in the sun we prepare,
If there are planes to fly there
That's where we will be.
To the glorious 'Few' we will swear
If the call ever comes we'll be there,
So we proudly hail them,
We won't fail them,
Sons of the Lords of the Air.

Dick Hurran

That Thing

Remaining anonymous — for obvious reasons — this Fleet Air Arm officer leaves us in no doubt as to his personal feelings about the Barracuda.

Why should the unoffending sky,
Be tainted and corrupted by
This product of a twisted brain,
That's aeronautically insane,
This vile and hideous abortion,
Devoid of beauty and proportion,
That people call a Barracuda,
Whose form is infinitely cruder
Than any other scheme or plan
As yet conceived by mind of man.
To see it stagger into space
Would bring a blush upon the face,
Of the most hardened Pharisee
Within the aircraft industry.
But I suggest we don't decry
This winged horror of the sky;
But keep it 'til the War is won,
And then we'll all join in the fun.
Festoon the wings with fairy lights
And wheel it out on gala nights,
Thus so we'll help dispel the rumour
That Britons have no sense of humour.

Anon. F.A.A. Officer

Night Bombers

From the flat lands of the Fens they took-off. Most of us never even knew that they had gone, until we read next day of those who never came back.

Eastward they climb, black shapes against the grey
Of falling dusk, gone with the nodding day
From English fields.
                                        Not theirs the sudden glow
Of triumph that their fighter-brothers know;
Only to fly through cloud, through storm, through night
Unerring, and to keep their purpose bright,
Nor turn until, their dreadful duty done,
Westward they climb to race the awakened sun.

The Gallant Sixty Two

No. 62 (Transport) Squadron flew Dakotas in Burma during 1944-1945. Pride of squadron comes through very strongly in their song which is sung to the tune of "The Road to the Isles"

Oh they flapped and they panicked in the arid Arakan,
They were cut off and they knew not what to do,
For the Japs had out-manoeuvred them (a very subtle plan)
So they had to go and call on Sixty Two.

Chorus: We can fly in, supply them in, or drop them from the tow,
Though the weather and the Japs may bid us nay,
They will be alright, by day and night, wherever they may go,
For Sixty Two will always lead the way.

Then the Japs came a-prancing down the Manipuri Road,
And debouched into the narrow Imphal Plain,
The Brown Jobs were surrounded; when they realised they'd been Joed,
Well they had to call on Sixty Two again.

Chorus: We can fly them in, etc.

The Seventeenth from Tiddim — we sped them on their way,
The Fifth to plug the Imphal Gap we flew,
And ne'er in Britain's history can anybody say,
So much was done so quickly by so few.

Chorus: We can fly them in, etc.

Now Kabaw is a valley, Easy-Easy a D.Z.,
Where the circuits we admit were rather wide,
Till the Jap one early morning thought he'd show his yellow head,
And shot down two by cutting round inside.

Chorus: We can fly them in, etc.

Through rain and cloud and anything you'll always find us game,
Bumps and pockets, hills in mist are our delight,
This last we proved convincingly with devastating aim,
On the man who waved the flag upon Fort White.

Chorus: We can fly them in, etc.

The Fourteenth reached the Chindwin where they built a Bailey Bridge,
Which we shot up very nicely every day,
Like flying fish we followed them, o'er every ruddy ridge,
And set them on the road to Mandalay.

Chorus: We can fly them in, etc.

From Shwebo to Meiktila, Pyinmanu to Rangoon,
The railways gave our aircrews quite a line,
And we'll fly by day and evening and any bomber's moon,
Till Nippons' Rising Sun sets in decline.

Chorus: We can fly them in, etc.

For its lifts and drops and casualties, and men and mules and
post,
Forever till the last trump sounds review,
When Saint Peter fights the devil and calls the Holy Ghost,
Why he'll travel in a kite from Sixty Two.

Chorus: We can fly them in, etc.

To the Men of my Squadron

Comradeship is the shining light in the darkness of war and it shone very brightly among the aircrews of Bomber Command.

Finest of mortal friends, I'll not forget
When war's a faded memory in the land
Which once stood tensely in the closing net,
I'll think of what is past — and understand.

Yours was a truthful voice among the lies,
Unshaken by the falsehoods that were rife
You were the men with level, fearless eyes
Who lived with death, yet still believed in life.

Laughter was yours, that held no bitter sting,
That bubbled up more quickly than the rest.
Your steady friendship was a sacred thing
And I who held it was doubly blessed.

Decades of easy peace may go their way
And tide and time will drift us far apart—
But you who shared our savage Yesterday,
Will hold the highest places in my heart.

F/Lt Peter Roberts

GLOSSARY

Ace Title originally given to French and American airmen in World War One who had five or more aerial victories. The British authorities have never officially recognised this title.

A.F.C. Air Force Cross.

Albatri The R.F.C.'s plural of Albatros.

A.O.C. Air Officer Commanding. Senior officer commanding an R.A.F. group.

Archie R.F.C. nickname for German anti-aircraft fire, taken from a line of a World War One musical comedy song, "Archibald, certainly not!"

A.T.A. Air Transport Auxiliary. World War Two civilian organisation for ferrying service aircraft.

A.T.C. Air Training Corps. A cadet corps which gives pre-service training to future R.A.F. personnel.

Avro A.V. Roe & Co. Ltd. One of the earliest aircraft manufacturers whose designs over the years ranged from the 504 to the Lancaster.

Attack American designation given to their light bomber squadrons.

Balloonatics Unofficial name for those who went aloft suspended from observation balloons in World War One.

Beau Bristol Beaufighter. Two-seat, twin-engined night and anti-shipping fighter.

Big Ack Aircrew name for the Armstrong Whitworth

F.K.8 two-seater, 1917-18. It was popular with its crews.

Bind R.A.F. slang, meaning to grumble or complain. Any awkward or dangerous job was a bind.

Black Cone An old air traffic signal which denoted unfavourable flying conditions

Bolo "Bolo House" (Hotel Cecil) was the R.F.C.'s London H.Q. Thus a bolo job was a safe one.

Burton "Gone for a Burton". A too-casual remark meaning that someone had been killed.

'Bus R.F.C. and R.A.F. slang for aeroplane.

C.F.I. Chief Flying Instructor. The "high priest" of a flying training school who, in the trainees' eyes, ranked second only to the Monarch in his importance.

Circuit Flight pattern round an airfield consisting of four ninety degree turns.

Cirrus High fleecy cloud.

Colney Hatch A hospital for the mentally sick.

Cubit An old measurement of length, about 18 inches.

Demobbed Short for demobilisation i.e., the release from the services of non-regular personnel.

D.F.C. Distinguished Flying Cross.

D.H. Initials preceeding numbers/names of all de Havilland aircraft, the most famous of a long line being the D.H.2, D.H.4., Tiger Moth and Mosquito.

Dims To take a "dim" (poor) view of something i.e., a duty, which is very disagreeable to the viewer!

D.S.C. Distinguished Service Cross.

D.Z. Dropping zone for troops, supplies etc.

Erk R.A.F. slang for a member of ground staff.

Eytie Services name for an Italian.

Fleet Air Arm The Royal Navy's air arm.

Flight A unit of three or more aircraft.

Fokker Famous series of German World War One aircraft, designed by the Dutchman, Anthony Fokker, the best marks being the E. III, the Dr. I Triplane and the D. VII.

Gen R.A.F. slang meaning information. "Pukkha gen" was the genuine information and "duff gen" was incorrect or useless.

Gremlins Imaginary characters who were seen only by aircrews, who blamed them for many mishaps.

Handley Page Manufacturers of heavy bombers from the 0/100 (World War One) to the Halifax (World War Two.)

Hun British name for a German and, paradoxically, the R.F.C's name for a pupil pilot.

K.B.E. Knight Commander of the Order of the British Empire.

Kite R.F.C., R.N.A.S. and R.A.F. slang for aeroplane.

Link An excellent simulated instrument flying trainer, named after its American designer.

Major Rank of R.F.C. squadron commanders.

M.C. Military Cross. Awarded to officers of the R.F.C.,

and still awarded to army officers.

Met Meteorological. Met man — weather forecaster.

N.B.G. No Bloody Good.

Nine 'A' D.H.9A. World War One two-seat day bomber and successor to the D.H.4.

Omer Drome St. Omer aerodrome. H.Q., R.F.C. in France.

P.B.O. Poor Bloody Observer (World War One). Observers came in all ranks from Air Mechanic and Private to Major.

P.R.U. Photographic Reconnaissance Unit.

R.A.F. Royal Aircraft Factory (World War One) and Royal Air Force (from 1 April 1918).

R.A.F.V.R. Royal Air Force Volunteer Reserve.

R.Aux.A.F. Royal Auxiliary Air Force.

R.C.A.F. Royal Canadian Air Force.

R.F.C. Royal Flying Corps.

Rigger R.A.F. tradesman, an expert in the rigging of aircraft.

R.N.A.S. Royal Naval Air Service.

Ropey R.A.F. slang — below standard or inferior.

Scout Official name for a single-seat fighter of World War One.

Ships American term for aircraft.

Stringbag Affectionate name for the Fairey Swordfish.

U.S.A.A.F. United States Army Air Forces.

Wimpey Airmen's name for the Vickers Wellington bomber, various marks of which gave excellent service throughout World War Two.

Wizard R.A.F. slang meaning superb, without equal.

V.C. Victoria Cross.

INDEX OF FIRST LINES